HOLIDAY HERO

HOLIDAY HERO

A MAN'S MANUAL FOR HOLIDAY LIGHTING

By Brad Finkle

CHRONICLE BOOKS
SAN FRANCISCO

Text copyright ©2003, 2007 Brad Finkle

Illustrations copyright ©2007 Joel Holland

Library of Congress Cataloging-in-Publication Data available.

ISBN-10: 0-8118-5637-2

ISBN-13: 978-0-8118-5637-9

Manufactured in China

Designed by Headcase Design

Distributed in Canada by Raincoast Books

9050 Shaughnessy Street

Vancouver, British Columbia V6P 6E5

10 9 8 7 6 5 4 3 2 1

Chronicle Books LLC

680 Second Street

San Francisco, California 94107

www.chroniclebooks.com

To my parents, who got me started in the business early in life by taking me around to all the local homes at Christmas, showing me the beauty and happiness that lights bring to the holidays.

To the memory of my father, who gave up many a hot meal so that all the power our house could supply at Christmas went to the elaborate displays outside our home, year after year.

And to Thomas, for unconditional love and support for the past 15 years.

SANTA'S LEGAL DISCLAIMERS

1. Lights run on electricity, and electricity is dangerous. So be careful, take your time, and remember: If you think something might be dangerous, it probably is.

2. Follow the manufacturer's instructions and specifications on lights, ladders, and other equipment you use. The author and Creative Decorating don't know what equipment you're dealing with, the unique conditions of your building or yard, or whether your hands are wet (they shouldn't be!), so the author, Creative Decorating, and the publisher do not warrant that all necessary safety information is provided here or elsewhere, nor does the author warrant that the procedures described here or elsewhere will lead to a successful or safe conclusion to any decorating carried out.

3. Neither the author nor Creative Decorating are forcing you to climb any ladder or undertake any particular project. This book provides ideas and information for you to consider. USE AT YOUR OWN RISK. By conducting any of the procedures in this book, you are taking full responsibility for your actions and absolving the author, Creative Decorating, and any other associated parties from all liability associated with such actions on your part. The author, Creative Decorating, and the publisher expressly disclaim any liability from any injury that may result from the use, proper or improper, of the instructions contained in this book, and they do not guarantee that the information contained herein is complete, safe, or accurate. The information in this book is provided "as is," with no warranties offered for accuracy or reproducibility.

4. Use your common sense and good judgment. You should fully assess the implication of using the information provided before actually utilizing the information.

5. Have a happy and safe holiday.

Contents

INTRODUCTION

It's that time of year again. You can't find a decent spot in the mall parking lot. You can't find a bank teller who isn't wearing a Santa hat. And you can't walk through the aisles of a grocery store without having someone almost drop a frozen turkey on your toe.

Yes, it's the holiday season—time to fatten the bonus check of the utility company's president by hanging as many lights as possible on your home. But that doesn't mean you have to go about it all willy-nilly. Not at all. That's where this book comes in. You're a man, dammit, and you want to make your home and yard the envy of the neighborhood, not the poster house for Citizens Against Lighting Fiascos. That guy in the red suit gets all the press, but you wear the pants in your house and you've got a job to do. If you don't do your job, Christmas doesn't come.

In these pages, you'll find everything you need to accomplish the most important task of the holiday season. But first, some words to light by. Corporations have mission statements; superheroes have solemn creeds—and now, so do you.

THE HOLIDAY HERO'S CREED

- I am a responsible light hanger and will not embarrass my family with a theme of purple lights just because I found them on sale.

- I will not shine floodlights into my neighbors' windows, unless they still haven't returned the cordless drill they borrowed last summer.

- I will meticulously wrap my extension cords so they won't end up in knots only an Eagle Scout could unwind.

- I will not put red-and-white hats on my yard gnomes, because yard gnomes are not elves.

- I will not ignore the warning label and use the top rung of my ladder as a step.

- I will not incorporate Santa Claus into a nativity scene or have him dancing on a dreidel.

- Most important, I will keep the number of lights I hang to less than six digits, and the amount I spend below the GNP of a South Pacific island nation. In short, I will resist the temptation to light my house so that on a clear night it's visible from the moon.

- I will also do my best not to give the electric company's meter reader dirty looks in January.

All right, enough introduction. Let the elves make their toys, let the womenfolk bake their pies. You're a Holiday Hero, and it's time to hang some lights.

{ FUSE BOX *see page 16* }

Chapter 1

THE BASICS

Let's take a moment to appreciate technological progress. Think about the Holiday Heroes of yore, out there lighting candles and lanterns every night. Electronic advances have made your job a little easier, but that doesn't mean you don't need to exercise a little savvy and take a few safety precautions. In this chapter, you'll learn to assemble a manly holiday tool kit, bone up on some electrical basics, and get to know your lights and accessories in and out.

HOLIDAY TOOL KIT

This is the best part of decorating—new tools. It's not too often that you are given permission to purchase new tools for a project, so let's take advantage of this, guys. Even if you don't need any tools for a certain project, you can always stock up for the year ahead. How about that power washer you always wanted? A nice, clean, power-washed home is a great starting point for your holiday decorating. Right, guys?

We know, of course, that you probably already have everything you need for any project. But, just in case, here's a list of tools to start with. Feel free to add to it as necessary.

THE MAN'S TOOL LIST FOR DECORATING

- 6-foot stepladder
- Extension ladder
- Extension ladder boots (rubber caps that slip over the tops of the ladder legs to prevent them from scratching that new paint or siding on your home)
- Extension pole
- Drill and masonry bit
- Screw eyes and plastic anchors
- Glue gun and, of course, glue sticks
- Electrical tape
- Duct tape

ELECTRICITY 101

The electrical outlets you plug your holiday lights into are very important. Many recently-built houses have outdoor outlets in both the front and rear of the home, as well as in the garage. This may sound like plenty, but there's one problem: these outlets are rarely on a circuit all by themselves. Indoor lights and outlets—even an entire section of your house—might be sharing the same circuit as your outdoor receptacles. So when you're testing holiday lights during the day, they may work fine. But add a few lights turned on inside after sunset and—boom!—there goes a breaker or fuse. If this happens, you'll need to spread your holiday lights around to other circuits to take the load off of those that tripped. Never reset a breaker or fuse without first taking some of the load off of the tripped circuit or finding out what made it trip.

KNOW YOUR POWER SOURCE

Not a member of the International Brotherhood of Electrical Workers? Not to worry. On the next few pages are a few definitions that should come in handy as you read through this book and prepare to install your holiday lights.

AMP: Short for ampere, the standard unit for measuring the strength of an electrical current, or its amperage. A typical household circuit carries 15 to 50 amps. If you open up the fuse/breaker panel in your home, you'll find the amperage printed on the face of each fuse or breaker. This number represents the maximum amperage you can draw from that circuit.

BREAKER/FUSE: A safety device that automatically interrupts the flow of electric current when that current becomes overloaded or a short circuit occurs. The number found on a breaker or a fuse is the maximum amperage that particular circuit can handle. When you plug too many items into your outlets and all these outlets are wired together (making a circuit) to the same breaker, the breaker trips (turns off), telling you that the power required to run these items is more than the breakers can handle. Older homes may have a fuse box instead of a breaker panel, with each round fuse representing a circuit in your home.

CIRCUIT: A complete path over which an electrical current can flow. The average home will have a circuit for each room; sometimes a circuit will cover more than one area of a home.

GROUND FAULT CIRCUIT INTERRUPTER (GFCI): A special outlet that shuts off power whenever it senses small electrical-current imbalances caused by a leakage to the ground, thus preventing electric shock. Homes built since the early 1980s have GFCIs on all outdoor outlets, as well as inside the home

anywhere there's a sink—bathroom, kitchen, laundry room—just in case you wake up and try to brush your teeth with a hair dryer before having that first cup of coffee. GFCIs don't replace fuses or breakers since they won't necessarily shut off if there's an overload or short circuit. However, moisture getting into the circuit that's on the GFCI should trip the outlet, shutting off the electricity to it. GFCI outlets have two buttons: "Test" and "Reset." If the GFCI is tripped, pushing the reset button will return the outlet to the circuit.

If you lose power and your breakers/fuses look okay, it's probably a tripped GFCI. Locating a tripped GFCI outlet can be tricky, though, since one GFCI can cover several non-GFCI outlets. Some homes even have the GFCI built into the breaker on your electrical panel. If you're not sure of the outlet that's tripped, start with the outside outlets. If those aren't the problem, move inside to the area where the power is out and check the bathroom, kitchen, or laundry room.

OUTLET (OR RECEPTACLE): Any point in a wiring system at which electrical current can be used by inserting a plug.

HOW MANY AMPS DOES ONE MAN NEED?

This chart should help you estimate the number of amps your light display will use, so that you can distribute the load across multiple outlets/circuits and not spend all your time resetting breakers or changing fuses. Of course, with all the different sizes and wattages of bulbs available, there's no way to give completely accurate estimates. But this is a good start.

LIGHTING	AMPS
50-bulb miniature-light set	0.17
100-bulb miniature-light set	0.34
150-bulb miniature net-light set	0.4
150-bulb miniature icicle-light set	0.4
20-foot rope light	0.9
150-watt floodlight	1.25
C7 25-foot strand	1.5
C9 25-foot strand	1.8

These are just examples of some of the different light con-figurations you're likely to encounter when you're out shopping. Watts measure the amount of electrical power needed to light the bulb and how bright the bulb is. The most popular lightbulbs you use in your home, for example, come in 60-watt, 75-watt, and 100-watt versions. Common wattages for Christmas lights are 5 or 7 watts for C7 bulbs, and 7 or 10 watts for C9 bulbs. Some packaging tells you what the wattage of the bulbs is—just remember, more watts equals brighter lights.

GEAR AND ACCESSORIES

There are almost as many accessories for holiday decorating as there are elves in Santa's workshop. In some cases you can use things you might already have laying around the house, and in other cases you'll have to go out and buy new gadgets to help make your house the envy of every aspiring Holiday Hero on your block. It's probably a good idea to wait to buy anything until after you've sketched out your plan—otherwise you might end up with a whole carload of net lights and no place to hang them.

EXTENSION CORDS

You probably have a couple of extension cords in your garage right now. Heck, you probably have a couple dozen. But when using them, try to match colors to the environment. For instance, if you're running a cord up a tree, use brown. The last thing your neighbors want to look at is a Day-Glo orange cord hanging in your yard all winter.

Make sure your cords are marked either medium- or heavy-duty, and that they're designed for outdoor use. But don't worry about brand names. Manufacturers have to meet specific safety requirements by law, so no one cord is better than any other. Cords can be found at any home-improvement store. If you're not sure exactly what type to buy, you can always ask a salesperson for assistance. Just make sure to explain your intended use for these cords, which should make your decision to pick up 15 or 20 cords seem a little less crazy.

In addition to plenty of extension cords, you'll also need to invest in a few extension-cord accessories, all of which are also available at home-improvement stores.

3-WAY ADAPTER: Lets you plug two or more cords into a single outlet.

3-TO-2 GROUNDING PLUG: Turns a three-prong male end into a two-prong male end when an outlet doesn't have a ground.

MALE AND FEMALE ENDS

It shouldn't be too hard to figure out which is which, but just in case: The male end has prongs, while the female end has an opening for a prong-headed male end. If you still have trouble sorting it out, give your TV's remote control to either the male or female end. The male end will change the channel to ESPN. The female end will switch to the Lifetime Network—or the Weather Channel if there's a storm within 200 miles.

MALE

FEMALE

PLASTIC LIGHT CLIPS

Whoever invented plastic light clips needs their own shrine in the Holiday Hero Hall of Fame. Thankfully, these little devices replaced the old hammer-and-nail-on-the-roofline technique several years ago. They can, quite frankly, take hours off your installation and takedown time. Constructed out of light, durable plastic, they won't damage your home's exterior. Look for ones labeled "All-In-One Clip." These hold pretty much any kind of strand, and will even hold individual C7 and C9 bulbs. To install, simply snap the light socket or light strand into the jaws of the clip and then slide the other clip end under your shingles or onto your gutters. Repeat as necessary, and that's it. Your lights are hung, and your thumb survives any errant hammering. Clips aren't just for roof-lines, either. Gutters, siding, even decks—they can all benefit from the genius of the anonymous clip developer. The clips are available where holiday lights are sold.

ADVANTAGES:

- Quick and easy to install
- Can hold both miniature lights and C7 and C9 bulbs
- Can be reused for several years

DISADVANTAGES:

- Clips can break during installation and take-down in very cold weather

LIGHT STAKES

These are ideal for lighting sidewalks, driveways, flowerbeds, or anything else on the ground. They're also very user-friendly, so you don't need a complicated 100-page manual explaining how to install them. All you need to do is take them out of the package, clip the light to the top of the stake, and push the stake into the ground. The hardest part is being on your knees when installing them (knee pads do help with these projects).

Light stakes can be made of either wire or mold-injected plastic. Most can handle any size light strand —from mini-lights to C9s. Look to the "All-In-One Light Stake" for the most versatility. Available where holiday lights are sold.

ADVANTAGES:

- Quick and easy to install
- Can be used with both miniature lights and C7 and C9 bulbs
- Reusable

DISADVANTAGES:

- Tough to install and take down if ground is too hard or frozen
- People and animals can trip on the stakes and cords

BLACKOUT CAPS

Perfect for covering the section of a light strand that stretches between two bushes lighted by the same strand, between two windows lighted by the same strand, or beyond the edge of your home's eaves. These caps slip over most miniature lightbulbs, completely blocking illumination from any section of a light strand that you want to keep dark. Available where holiday lights are sold.

ADVANTAGES:

- Work on most brands of miniature lights
- Hide the light completely
- Easy to install and reusable

DISADVANTAGES:

- A little hard to remove from the bulb

OUTDOOR TIMERS

Forget turning your lights on every night—let a timer take care of it for you. There are three types of timers available.

PHOTOCELL: Turns on at dusk via a light sensor. You can usually set these to turn off after a specific time period so that your lights don't blaze all night.

CONVENTIONAL/MANUAL: These have a dial in the center, and tabs that you place on the times you want your lights to turn on and off. They're available in 10- and 15-amp capacity.

DIGITAL: La-di-da. The ultimate in ease—at least once you've got them programmed.

ADVANTAGES:
- You don't even have to be home to turn the lights on or off
- With programmable versions, you can set the exact time you want the lights to turn on and off

DISADVANTAGES:
- If there's a power failure, you'll need to reset the manual timers
- Setting multiple timers to turn on simultaneously can be a challenge

Unless you're comfortable with technology, stick with the outdoor 15-amp conventional timer.

HINT

SNAP-TOGETHER WINDOW FRAME FOR MINI-LIGHTS

These frames are durable PVC plastic strips that you can cut to fit windows of any size or shape—inside or outside. Once you size the strips to fit the sides of your window, just snap them together to create a frame. Then insert your mini-lights and place the frame in the window. This means no more nails or staples in your woodwork, which means future potential homebuyers won't say, "Look, nails and staples in the woodwork." Available at most places where holiday lights are sold.

ADVANTAGES:
- Can be installed without damaging woodwork
- Reinstallation takes just minutes
- Looks picture-perfect when illuminated

DISADVANTAGES
- Very time-consuming to put together the first time
- Larger windows require extra reinforcement of the frame

EXTENSION POLE

If you plan on decorating that 15-foot evergreen in your yard, put the ladder back in the garage. Using an extension pole with a light-hanging attachment is the only safe way to go about hanging decorations on trees. Working from the ground also gives you a better perspective on what you're lighting. Check the paint department at a home-improvement store for the poles—they come in lengths of 6 to 24 feet—and then head to the holiday lighting department to pick up your light-hanging attachment.

ADVANTAGES:

- Safer than hanging off a ladder
- Makes installation and takedown of lights quicker
- Gives you big-picture perspective while installing lights

DISADVANTAGES:

- Poles can be a little awkward and heavy when fully extended
- No more excuses for not decorating the really tall trees in your yard

METAL CLIPS/SCREW EYES

Putting decorations right onto your brick or stone home is no longer a problem. For brick homes, you have two options. You can use metal clips that snap snugly over the face of the brick and can hold up to 15 pounds. Or you can install anchors and screw eyes. These require a drill, a masonry drill bit, a plastic anchor, and a metal screw eye. Consider these permanent fixtures on your home that can be used for other holiday decorations, too. If you own a stone house, anchors and screw eyes are the only way to go. Either way, you'll find everything you need at your local home-improvement center.

METAL CLIPS

ADVANTAGES:

- Quick to install and remove
- No tools necessary

DISADVANTAGES:

- Less sturdy than a permanent hook installed in the wall
- A strong wind can blow items off the clip
- Weight limitations

SCREW EYES

ADVANTAGES:

- Can hold heavy decorations when properly installed
- Will hold decorations in place during high winds
- Quick reinstallation

DISADVANTAGES:

- Requires drilling holes into your house
- Initial installation takes a little longer

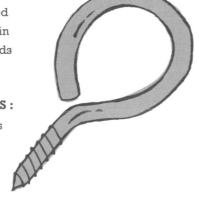

LIGHTS, DECORATIONS, ACTION

Maybe your plan is to sleep in on Sunday, spend an hour hanging a few old light strands you found in the basement, and by two o'clock be in your Barcalounger drinking beer. Nothing wrong with that plan, but let's just say it won't win you any awards. This is the fun part. Christmas lights and decorations come in a dizzying array of colors, shapes, and sizes. Take a few minutes to familiarize yourself with what's available in the world of outdoor lighting and holiday decor, and I guarantee you'll add instant panache to your presentation. Remember, always follow the manufacturer's directions on the package.

MINIATURE LIGHTS

In the late '70s, the backlash against disco and OPEC's rising energy costs converged. The result? Mini-lights. The most efficient type of lights to operate, mini-lights now dominate the holiday market. Miniature-light strings are the most versatile lighting accessory on the market today, adding that special glow anyplace you install them. What else can turn that dead tree or bush in your yard into a living, glowing sparkle of life that everyone can enjoy? Their uses are unlimited—inside or outside, on bushes, trees, walkways, rooflines, even the family schnauzer (if you can get him to keep still).

Most mini-light strings have a male plug with a fuse at one end and a female receptacle at the other. This lets you easily string them together. You'll find them in 50-, 100-, or 200-light strings. The 50s are simply too short, and the 200s get tangled and are hard to manage during installation and takedown. Trust me and go with the 100-light strings. And look for lights with a lamp-lock system. These lock the individual bulbs into place to ensure good connections. Depending on manufacturer and style, you can usually string three 100-light sets in a row. Any more and you risking a blown fuse at the male end of the first strand.

ADVANTAGES:

- More energy-efficient and less expensive than bigger bulbs
- Versatile and easy to work with
- Sold everywhere

DISADVANTAGES:

- Most minis are wired in a series, which means broken or burned bulbs break the circuit and cause part of the string not to work
- Careful installation and takedown required to avoid breaking or dislodging bulbs
- Need to replace burned-out bulbs to keep the set working

C7 AND C9 LIGHTS

The predecessors of mini-lights, C7 and C9 strands aren't as prevalent these days as they were during the Nixon/Ford administration. Nonetheless, they're still out there and easily brighten any roofline or large outdoor evergreen. Just like minis, these light strands have a male and female end so that you can string them together. However, they usually come in 25-light sets. You'll find the bulbs are primarily either ceramic or transparent (see-through) and come in a variety of colors. Depending on the manufacturer, you can usually string three 25-light sets in a row for a total of 7.5 feet. These larger bulbs are best used for lighting large areas that need lots of illumination, where a miniature-light string would not be visible enough—to trim your house, for example, or on large trees. They also work perfectly with light stakes.

ADVANTAGES:

- Wired in parallel, which means one burned or loose bulb won't cause an entire string to go out
- The brightest type of Christmas light
- Male plugs contain replaceable fuses for overload protection

DISADVANTAGES:

- Require more power than miniature lights
- Bulbs become very hot
- More expensive to purchase and operate than mini-lights

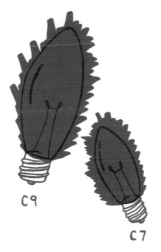

C9

C7

NET LIGHTS

Just as the name suggests, these lights are uniformly spaced into a preformed grid, or "net." They have the same effect as the other miniature-light strings, but with fewer headaches. They're ideal for wrapping around a tree trunk or treetop, or for simply laying over your front-yard flora like a blanket to provide uniform lighting.

Net lights have a male plug in one corner and a female receptacle in the opposite corner, so that you can string together up to three sets. Square, tapered, and triangular shapes are available, with clear or colored lights. If you're looking for that fast install, then these lights are for you. They take just minutes to hang. Simply take them out of the box, unfold them, lay them on that bush or hedge, and plug them in.

ADVANTAGES:

- Tangle-free and uniformly spaced
- Easy to install and take down
- Three display modes—steady, blinking, and chasing (motion)

DISADVANTAGES:

- More expensive than regular mini-lights
- Like minis, they're wired in a series, which means broken or burned bulbs break the circuit and cause a section of the net not to work
- Because they're available in a limited range of sizes, it may be hard to perfectly cover your shrubbery

ROPE LIGHTS

Fairly new on the circuit (so to speak), rope lights contain a series of lights spaced an inch apart, all wrapped in a durable PVC tube. Fully flexible, they offer almost endless possibilities inside or out, framing windows, porches, or doorways. They're sold in lengths of 10 to 150 feet and are easily cut to specific lengths. There are many accessories available, including power connectors, T-connectors, end caps, and mounting clips. When seen at night, rope lights look like a continuous stream of lights in a tube. These

lights are harder to install in a precise alignment and require more time to set up than C7 or C9 bulbs. They're best used for wrapping around tree trunks, railings, or even through wreaths and garland for a special look.

ADVANTAGES:

- Bulbs will not fall out or come loose
- Can be displayed in steady, blinking, or chasing (motion) mode

DISADVANTAGES:

- More expensive than miniature-light sets and C7 or C9 strands
- Only way to replace burned-out bulbs is to cut the section out and replace it (most rope lights can be cut to predetermined lengths)

FLOODLIGHTS AND SPOTLIGHTS

The rock stars of the lighting world, floodlights and spotlights can focus on a particular display in the yard, a wreath on your house, or a spectacular tree. Depending on the intended use, you can buy either a floodlight (which casts a wide beam of light) or a spotlight (which throws a narrow beam). You'll find a wide range of wattages—from 25 to 175—and many different colors. Be careful, though. Even outside, 175 watts is a heckuva lot of light. And make sure to buy only lights and light sockets intended for outdoor use.

ADVANTAGES:

- Quick and easy to install
- Capable of lighting large areas
- Available in different sizes and colors

DISADVANTAGES:

- Hard to focus on smaller areas
- Floodlights sometimes give an unprofessional look
- Snow can cover the illumination from a floodlight or spotlight

ICICLE LIGHTS

Saying that these lights are popular is like saying January in Buffalo, New York, is "kind of cold." They're everywhere. And for good reason: they really are beautiful when hung well. Rooflines are the obvious choice for icicle lights, but don't pass up fences, decks, and walkways. Easily strung together with their male and female ends, icicle lights are commonly found in 8- to 10-foot-long strings with white or green wire and vertical drops of up to 26 inches. White wire works best in most situations, and the longer the vertical drop the better. Originally made with clear lights only, you can now find them in a variety of colors, too.

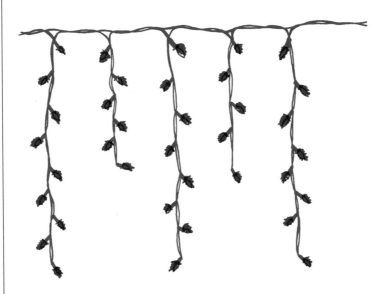

When hanging them from the roofline, don't forget your plastic clips (see page 22). A good rule: no less than one clip for every six inches of lights.

ADVANTAGES:

- Preformed vertical drops
- Easy to attach with plastic clips
- Can be displayed in steady or blinking modes

DISADVANTAGES:

- Like minis, they're wired in a series
- Dangling bulbs are more prone to breaking
- Wind can blow the lights onto your roof or into your gutters

WHAT TO SPEND

The better the quality of the lights, the more you'll pay. If you're in the Witness Protection Program and regularly leave your belongings behind in a hurry, go ahead and buy cheap lights. Everyone else should probably spring for at least the mid-range lights. In the long run, they're actually less expensive because you don't need to replace them as often.

There are three different grades of miniature-light strings sold in the United States:

LOW. Found at discount department stores and some hobby stores, these light sets sell for less than $2 for a 100-bulb set.

MEDIUM. These can be purchased at home-improvement and hardware stores for $4 to $7 per 100-bulb set.

HIGH. Sold at nurseries and specialty Christmas stores, these lights cost around $12 to $18 per set of 100. Some are called "commercial" sets.

So, what is the best choice when buying light sets? That is the $64,000 question. For sure, don't buy the low-grade lights (unless you plan to throw them away at the end

continued ▶

of the season), and the high-grade ones aren't worth the money. So, that leaves the medium-grade.

Also, consider not just the number of lights but also the actual length of the strand. You know how you could buy a 24-ounce bag of potato chips for $1.99 a couple years back, and now a bag of chips sells for the same price even though it's just a 19-ounce bag? Well, the Christmas-light manufacturers are doing the same thing. Two years ago, a set of 100 miniature lights was 46 feet long; today it's just 33 feet long. If you have a choice and a lot of lighting to take care of, all other things being equal, go with the longest strand available. And make sure there's a female plug at the end of the light set if you need to plug another set into it.

WREATHS

A simple wreath lit by a spotlight or a strand of mini-lights easily adds a touch of elegance to your display. Though many people go with natural wreaths, you might want to consider a high-quality artificial wreath for outdoors. No one will ever know, and you'll never have to pay for another wreath again. They come in diameters of 24 to 72 inches, and you can buy them plain, prelit, or fully decorated. Hang them over your front door or garage doors to welcome visitors to your Annual Eggnog Extravaganza.

YARD DECORATIONS

If you want a focal point in your display, try yard decorations. These days, virtually any kind of decorative object is available— candy canes, deer, snowflakes, Santas, and Stars of David, to name just a few. We wouldn't be surprised if you could find a grandma getting run over by a reindeer. And if you can't find exactly what you want, you can always build it with a wire frame or wooden cutouts. (Consider keeping your yard decorations close to the house to discourage the Humbugs from vandalizing or stealing them.)

If you were to do an Internet search for "Christmas decorations" you would find more than two million different sites that offer outdoor decorations for sale. That said, let's just focus on some of the more popular decorations people are using and not make this book War and Peace–size.

BLOW MOLDS

Blow molds? Okay, what are blow molds? These are displays made of mold-injected plastic and illuminated by a light inside. Popular back in the 1970s, they can still be found where Christmas decorations are sold—right behind all the new yard accessories available. They come in many different sizes and styles, from miniature ones for windows to life-size ones that require two people to set up. Any freestanding blow mold should be weighted down with rocks or sand, or even secured with landscaping nails, so that a strong wind won't blow it into Mr. Scrooge's yard. Some of the most common blow molds are of Santa, reindeer, and snowmen.

INFLATABLES

In the last couple of years, these blow-up lighted displays made of fabric have started popping up in more and more yards. You now can find inflatables everyplace you shop. Available for every single holiday you can imagine—and even some holidays that don't exist!—they come in several different sizes, representing any character you can name. If you have never had the experience of seeing an inflatable up close, they are pretty cool. They have a fan on the bottom of the figure; when plugged into an outlet, the fan turns on and the display comes to life. When the power is turned off, the display deflates and lies on the ground until the power gets turned on again. The majority of the inflatable displays have a light inside of them to illuminate the whole figure when it's plugged in. To set up your display, all you have to do is unpack your inflatable from the small box it comes in, plug it into an outlet, stake it down in the yard (stakes are supplied)—and that's it! And when the holidays are over, just put it right back in the box it came in and store it till next year comes around.

WIRE-FRAME SCULPTURES

Wire-frame sculptures are another type of yard decoration that has been growing in popularity over the last few years. Most of these displays are made out of 1/4-inch-round wire shaped into a frame, which is painted and decorated with miniature lights to make up a figure. The majority of these sculptures are designed to be placed in the yard. There are also some that can be hung from the side of your house, and others that are three-dimensional and can be hung from trees.

Most stores that sell Christmas decorations now also sell an assortment of these wire-frame displays. They are easy to install—just unpack, assemble (if necessary), find a location for the display, attach it to the ground, and plug it in. Most of these sculptures have legs that you can push into the ground to hold them up, and some come with stakes to hammer into the ground. Some of these need a little more staying power, though—tie them to wooden stakes or a metal T-post for maximum support.

GARLAND

Garland normally comes in 9-foot lengths. Thickness and colors vary (the thicker the garland, the nicer-looking it will be on your home), as do decorative options. Some garland is plain, some has lights, and some has more decorations than you can shake a candy cane at. Check your local hobby or arts-and-crafts store for a better selection than you'll find at discount stores or home-improvement centers. Today, artificial garland is just as real-looking as the real thing. When it comes to greenery for outside, artificial is the way to go—buy once and use over and over. You can purchase garland prelit, or add lights yourself. And don't forget to add a bow, too—these come premade, or you can be unique and make one yourself. For outdoors, lighted garland with a big red bow adds a lot of beauty to your display. Key locations for garland are over the front entryway to your home, on railings, around decks, on pillars, and even around the top of your garage.

You can easily add lights, bows, or pinecones to garland yourself. You'll need a 100-bulb mini-light strand for each nine-foot section of garland.

HINT

{ SKETCH YOUR PLAN *see page 50* }

Chapter 2

THE PLAN

A plan. Some lights. A gallon of your favorite holiday drink in the kitchen. It's time for The Show. Ready? Good. Let's get down to business. No matter how simple or complex your design, the first thing you'll need to do is make a sketch. It is the single most important step in designing your display. That bears repeating: Making a sketch is the single most important step in designing your display. It will save you time and money in the long run. And it can be a fun way to involve the whole family in the process, since you probably don't want your six-year-old up on the roofline with you. So let's talk sketches.

THE BASIC SKETCH

1. Get a piece of standard 8 $\frac{1}{2}$-by-11-inch paper and a pencil. Not a pen. Even the most decisive of us eventually changes his mind.
2. Grab a family member or two and walk to the front of your property to observe the full lay of the land.
3. Draw a rough sketch of your home and its surroundings. Include doors, driveways, walkways, trees, and bushes— essentially anything that you could use in your display. Start with the house itself and then add in the other elements.
4. Locate all outside outlets and make note of them on your sketch. In the front of the house, look near the porch. In the back, look near the back door. And don't forget about your garage.
5. Go back inside and grab a cup of your favorite holiday drink.

Now it's time for a little design. Discuss with your family exactly what you want to decorate. Think about lighting displays that have caught your eye over the years. How can you make yours better? Refer back to the "Lights, Decorations, Action" section in chapter 1, or skip ahead to chapter 4 for some inspiration. What kind of lights do you want to use? What sizes, styles, and colors? Do you want to have a theme? Snowmen? Reindeer? Keep in mind, it's not necessary to blow it out in your first year. By adding lights and decorations over time, you can spread out your lighting investment and make a bigger splash each successive season.

DESIGN GUIDELINES

1. Determine the focus of your display and decorate around it. Whether it's a specially made 100-inch wreath or an 8-foot inflatable snowman, let one thing shine, and everything else shines around it.

2. Design symmetrically. If you have lights on one side of the house, do something on the other side for balance.

3. Try to use only one or two colors of lights in your display. When you use more, it becomes less of a "display" and more "a whole bunch of holiday lights."

TAKING MEASUREMENTS

Now that you've decided what kinds of lights you want to use and have some design ideas in mind, it's time to head back outside. This time, bring along a measuring tape, a pencil, your sketch, and your helpers.

THE HOUSE

Measure the roofline, windows, doorways, walkways, and driveway—wherever you're hanging lights or greenery. And don't worry about using a ladder. You can take estimated measurements of the roofline and higher windows from the ground. You don't need 100 percent accuracy, just a close approximation. Make sure that one of your helpers is recording the dimensions on your sketch next to the appropriate features.

SHRUBS AND SMALL TREES

This includes bushes, hedges, small or medium evergreens, and trees less than 10 feet tall. For mini-lights, we suggest the "random lighting" technique. As the name suggests, you won't place the lights in any particular order for coverage. Whether you're using the minis or net lighting (or both), you'll need to measure each piece of greenery to get its area in square feet. This is easily accomplished by multiplying the height times the length for hedgerow-type bushes, or the height times the diameter for circular bushes and trees.

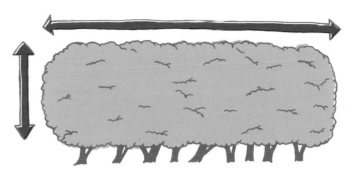

The chart on page 54 shows you how many 100-bulb mini-light sets you'll need for your shrubbery. A good rule of thumb is to use one 100-bulb set for every 15 square feet, though your personal taste may call for more or less.

If you're using net lights, you still need to know the total area you're dealing with so you can buy the appropriate sets. Net lights come in many different sizes, starting from 4 by 4 feet. To make sure you have your bushes covered, just multiply the two numbers on the box of the net lights (for example, 4 x 4 = 16) and compare that to the total area of your shrubs.

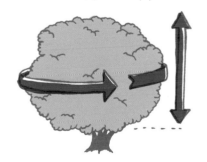

RANDOM LIGHTING

You've calculated the square footage of your trees and shrubs, now use this chart to calculate how many strands of mini-lights you'll need for the random lighting technique.

SQUARE FEET	100-BULB MINI-LIGHT SETS
Up to 15	1
16–30	2
31–45	3
46–60	4
61–75	5
76–90	6
91–105	7
106–120	8
121–135	9
136–150	10

MEDIUM-SIZE TREES (10 TO 15 FEET TALL)

With larger trees, you'll move out of the random lighting technique for the branches and into one of two other methods—spiral lighting or branch wrapping.

For spiral lighting, measure the tree's circumference at its widest point around (the whole tree including the branches, not just the trunk). This can be done from the ground, because, again, you don't need 100 percent accuracy. Multiply the tree's circumference by its height to figure out how many feet of lighting you'll need. For example: a tree that has a 10-foot circumference and 10-foot-tall body (from the lowest branches up) would need 100 feet of lights, with each row spaced about a foot apart.

For branch wrapping, you want to pick three or four main branches of the tree to highlight, and wrap them individually. In general, it's easier to wrap just the branches of larger trees than trying to cover the entire body. What's a little trickier is determining the exact number of lights you'll need, because no two branches are ever the same size. That's why we've included this handy chart, which shows the approximate number of 100-bulb mini-light sets you'll need to wrap the branches of your tree.

BRANCH WRAPPING

Determine the height of your tree; then use this chart to estimate how many sets of mini-lights you'll need.

HEIGHT OF TREE	100-BULB MINI-LIGHT SETS
5 feet	2
10 feet	3
15 feet	6
20 feet	9
25 feet	12
30 feet	15
35 feet	18
40 feet	21

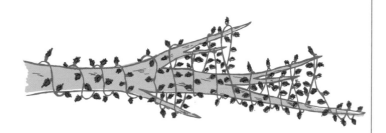

Wrapping the tree trunk, well, wraps up the tree lighting. The most practical way to wrap the trunk is with mini-lights. On average, you'll use one or two 100-light strings per trunk. Now, you can also use a fairly new product called a trunk net, although we don't recommend them because no two trunks are alike and the uniformity of the lights could be anything but uniform. Should you decide on trunk nets, however, just make sure you have the height and girth of the trunk written on your sketch. You'll need it when you're at the store.

LARGE EVERGREEN TREES

We highly recommend using the spiral technique with C7 or C9 strands to decorate larger pines and firs. Mini-lights tend to get lost in the branches and needles, not giving a very brilliant display. For spiral lighting measurements and techniques, see "Medium-Size Trees" on page 55.

C7 and C9 strands consume a lot more power than their mini-light counterparts. You'll need several extension cords and separate outlets for bigger jobs. See the "How Many Amps Does One Man Need?" chart on page 18.

After taking wreaths, garland, and yard decorations into consideration, your sketch should now look similar to this:

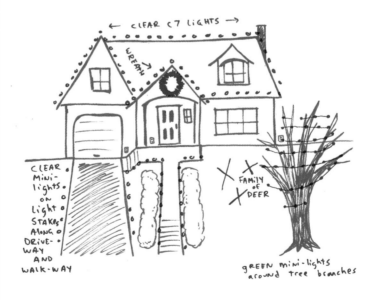

THE FINAL
MEASUREMENTS

The roofline's done, the shrubs are done, and the trees are done. Now it's just a matter of measuring for electrical supply. It's simple, really. Just measure the distance from the various outlets you'll use to the different light displays to determine how many cords and timers you'll need. Since every home is wired differently, it is impossible to generalize exactly how many amps are available at each of your outside outlets. If you don't have the electrical blueprints of your home and you're not a licensed electrician, the best advice for not overloading any one outlet is to distribute your display as equally as possible among all your available outside outlets. Look around your house to determine how many outlets are available to you.

If you are lighting the trim with the bigger bulbs (C7s or C9s), keep in mind that they use up to 10 times as much power as miniature lights, so they will need to be on their own outlets with nothing else plugged in. If you have just a couple of bushes with mini-lights or other small decorations needing power, run an extension cord to another free outlet. Larger displays just need to use more outlets—split the power among them the best you can. If your display turns into a national Christmas spectacle, you just might need to add a few more outside outlets to handle the power requirements. If your brother-in-law is a licensed electrician, you're set. If not, you'd better call a professional.

Looking at your sketch and the available outlets you have to work with, try to estimate how many extension cords you will need, using the outlet closest to each of the areas needing power. Note these lengths by updating your sketch. For example, say you have two outlets that you will be using for your display: one on the porch for lighting three different areas on the right side of the yard, and one in the garage for lighting three different areas on the left side of the yard. You don't need to run a separate extension cord for each of the three areas needing power. The majority of the time you can run one heavy extension cord from the outlet to the center of the area needing power and put a 3-way adapter (see page 21) on the end of the main cord and plug in all three areas into the end on the main line.

Finally, don't forget the finishing touch of adding a timer at each of the outlets you are using.

SHOPPING LIST

Keep track of all sizes and quantities of your supplies at the bottom of your sketch. Remember, having colored extension cords that blend into their surroundings will add to the beauty of your display. Now you are ready to start shopping—with the following checklist to help.

SHOPPING CHECKLIST

LIGHTS

Mini-Lights (100-bulb string)

Color_____ Qty_____

Color_____ Qty_____

Color_____ Qty_____

Color_____ Qty_____

C7 Lights (25-light strand)

Color_____ Qty_____

Color_____ Qty_____

Color_____ Qty_____

Color_____ Qty_____

C9 Lights (25-light strand)

Color_____ Qty_____
Color_____ Qty_____
Color_____ Qty_____
Color_____ Qty_____

Net Lights

Size_____ Color_____ Qty_____
Size_____ Color_____ Qty_____
Size_____ Color_____ Qty_____
Size_____ Color_____ Qty_____

Icicle Lights

Length needed _____ Color_____
Length needed _____ Color_____
Length needed _____ Color_____

Rope Lights

Length needed _____ Color_____ Qty_____
Length needed _____ Color_____ Qty_____
Length needed _____ Color_____ Qty_____
Length needed _____ Color_____ Qty_____

Floodlights/Spotlights

Watts_____ _____   Color_____   Qty_____

Watts_____   Color_____   Qty_____

Floodlight Fixture

Qty_____

ACCESSORIES

Plastic Light Clips (available in packages of 20 to 100)

Qty___ ___

Light Stakes (available in packages of 25 to 50)

Qty_____

Wreaths

Diameter_____   Qty_____

Diameter_____   Qty_____

Diameter_____   Qty_____

Garland

Length needed_____   Color lights_____
Length needed_____   Color lights_____
Length needed_____   Color lights_____

Bows

Color_____   Qty_____
Color_____   Qty_____
Color_____   Qty_____

YARD DECORATIONS

Inflatable

Character_____   Qty____
Character_____   Qty____
Character_____   Qty____

Blow Mold

Type_____   Size_____   Qty____
Type_____   Size_____   Qty____
Type_____   Size_____   Qty____
Type_____   Size_____   Qty____

Wire-Frame Sculpture

Type_____ Size_____ _____ Qty____

Type_____ Size_____ Qty____

Type_____ Size_____ Qty____

Type_____ Size_____ Qty____

TOOLS AND HARDWARE

Extension Pole/Light-Hanging Adapter

Masonry Drill Bit

Plastic Anchors

Screw Eyes

ELECTRICAL

Extension Cords (Brown)

Length_____ Qty_____

Length_____ Qty_____

Extension Cords (Green)

Length_____ Qty_____

Length_____ Qty_____

Extension Cords (White)

Length_____   Qty_____
Length_____   Qty_____

3-Way Adapter

Qty_____

3-to-2 Grounding Plugs

Qty_____

Timers

Qty_____

{ INSTALLING ALONG THE ROOFLINE *see page 72* }

Chapter 3

INSTALLATION

Congratulations. You can now wear your tool belt with pride. Almost. Because there's one thing you should do before you begin to install your display—unpack and test your lights inside. Carefully go over each strand before plugging it in. Look for broken or missing bulbs. Check for worn or cut wiring. And once you plug your lights in, check for bad bulbs again. With mini-lights or icicle lights, it will be fairly easy to tell if there's a bulb problem, since at least half of the strand will be out. With C7 and C9 strands, remember to inspect each bulb individually. And don't forget to thoroughly inspect your extension cords, as well. Don't use them if they're damaged.

If you come across a broken bulb, unplug the light string before putting in a replacement. When replacing a burned-out bulb, on the other hand, it's not necessary to unplug the light string first. Miniature lights can be removed by pulling them straight up out of the socket. With the bigger bulbs—C7s or C9s—you will need to unscrew the bulb from the socket and screw in a new one. If you do encounter a set of lights that just will not work, toss it out and buy a new set of lights. If this is a new set of lights you just purchased, return it and get a replacement.

Now you can finally grab your gear and head outside, right? As long as common sense has prevailed and you've put your decorating plans in a vinyl sheet protector to keep them from getting wet (so you can use them again next year), yes, you can go outside.

READY, SET, INSTALL!

STEP 1: LAY OUT YOUR EXTENSION CORDS

Starting with the extension cords may sound backward, but it's the way every professional does it. Why? When you're installing lights, you need to have them plugged in and working to make sure your connections are good and that your bulbs remain intact during installation. It can save you a lot of time—and frustration—in the long run.

So go outside and sort your cords by size and color, pairing them up with the necessary timers and extension-cord accessories. Now, look at your plan and start plugging them into the outlets you've selected. Always start by plugging your heaviest-gauge cord into the outlet. As you split off your cords to the different elements of your display, you can use smaller gauges. As you move away from the outlet, run your cord (or cords) across the grass, through the flower bed, under the fence—whatever you need to do to get the female end(s) where you need to plug in your lights. Remember to use the shortest cord that will do the job—you don't need a 50-foot cord if a 20-foot cord will do.

Covering plugs and connector joints with bags or tape doesn't protect them. In fact, it can trap moisture inside and cause electrical problems. Be sure your plugs and joints are safe for outdoor use.

ROOFLINE

Decide on the starting point for your lights by locating your power source. Start on the side closest to that source. Of course, depending on the types of lights you use and how long your roofline is, you may need more than one extension cord and power source. Wrapping the cord up around a drainpipe will hold the cord in place for the trim lights. For places that you can't reach, just leave the extension cords on the ground for right now.

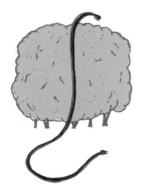

BUSHES AND HEDGES

Run the female end of the cord up into the middle of the bush or hedge, letting it lie on top or at least within reach. Wrapping the cord around a couple of branches will hold it in place until you plug in your lights. For really long bushes or hedges, you might want to add a 3-way adapter and run additional cords, evenly spaced, throughout the bush.

TREES

First, hang the female end of the cord from the lowest branch, close to the trunk. Leave about a foot hanging, because this cord is going to handle both the trunk lights and the lights on the body of the tree. After that, wrap the rest of the cord down around the trunk, nice and snug, before you plug it in.

EVERGREENS

If you have enough exposed trunk to work with, begin by hanging the female end of the cord from the lowest branch, close to the trunk (just like other trees), and wrap the rest of the cord down snugly around the trunk before you plug it in. If there's not any exposed trunk, wrap the female end of the cord around the outside of a branch at a good working height, and hide the cord inside the other branches as you work your way down before plugging it in.

LIGHT STAKES, YARD DECORATIONS, AND GREENERY

Referring to your plan, determine what other areas still need power. Then run cords to those locations. Try to use green cords in open areas—essentially any place people will see them. Use orange cords wherever you can hide them.

STEP 2: INSTALL THE LIGHTS

ROOFLINE

If your roofline is low, you may be able to use a stepladder. If not, plan on buying or borrowing an extension ladder. Make sure your ladders are in proper working condition, and always use them on stable ground. One of your helpers should always be there to provide support and to hand up supplies. Extension ladders should be placed at an angle that is comfortable and safe to climb. We have all seen the "miracle" extension poles in TV commercials that profess to make installing lights on the interior and exterior of your home easy, but though these look and sound great, there are way too many drawbacks to using them. Usually you have to buy special clips to attach the lights to them; they only extend about 15 feet; because they are made out of plastic, they are very flimsy and break easily; and it's impossible to get your lights evenly aligned when using them. Installing your roofline lights by hand is the only way to achieve a clean, professional look.

Start at the end of your house where your power is waiting for you on the ground. Try running your cords up to the trim along the backs of drainpipes—they make good hiding places. Now grab your plastic clips and the lights for the trim and climb on up (with a helper holding the ladder). Begin by installing the plastic clips, estimating the distance between each clip based on the length between bulbs on your light strand. Attach the lights to the clips, and push/slide the clips into final position, tightening the connecting wire between each pair of bulbs. Follow this procedure all the way around the area you're lighting. Remember to plug in the mini-lights first. With C7 or C9 strands, place the plug next to the cord, making sure it will reach; after finishing the install, plug them in and check for bad bulbs.

Whenever possible, work with mini-lights on. This way, if there's a problem with the string, you can fix it before proceeding. With C7s or C9s, on the other hand, work with the lights off. The filaments in these bulbs make them more fragile than mini-lights and more susceptible to burnout if shaken.

HINT

If you're installing icicle lights, remember that you can connect only a limited number of strings in a row—usually three sets (follow the manufacturer's directions on the package). If you need more than that, you will need to add on to your extension cord and run it along the trim so you can plug in the next string of lights. Follow this procedure all the way around the area you're lighting. Let's say, for example, that your trim will take six sets of lights. Since you can plug in only three sets end-to-end, you will need another power source to plug in your second set of three light sets. Do this by adding a 3-way adapter to the female end of the extension cord you're using for the trim and plugging in another extension cord that will run to the next set of lights.

HINT

As you finish up a section of your display, leave it plugged in and working. Leaving your display plugged in as you complete each section is a good way to make sure you're not overloading any single circuit. If you plug in your next set of lights and the breaker or fuse blows, you'll know you're using too much power and will need to transfer some of the cords to another circuit.

ATTACHING LIGHTS
TO BRICK OR STONE

No siding? You will need to use metal clips that snap snugly
over the faces of bricks. Or, grab your drill and a masonry
drill bit. Make a hole near each corner of the window or
doorway you're decorating. Drilling into the mortar between
bricks or stones is easier than drilling into the hard stuff
itself. (For more on metal clips and screw eyes, see the expla-
nation on pages 28 and 29.) Now push plastic anchors into
each hole, and then screw eyes into each anchor. Turn the
screw eyes so that the threads are completely inside the
anchors. You might need pliers for this. From this point, you
can just follow the directions for windows and doorways on
the next page.

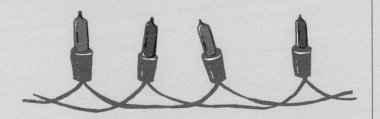

WINDOWS AND DOORWAYS

Plastic clips (page 22) and frames (page 27) are actually made for windows and doorways, so first try using those. If they don't work, use screw eyes at the corners of your windows and doors. Don't use staples or nails. Staples need to be removed, and after a few years of using them, you'll end up with siding that looks like Swiss cheese. Nails simply don't provide the

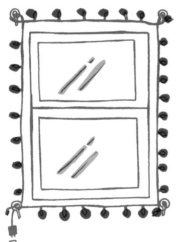

security needed for lights—one strong wind and your square window display becomes an oval, or even falls to the ground. You may need to open the screw eyes a little with a pair of pliers to get the strands all the way in. Wrap the strands once or twice through each eye, and follow the line of eyes around until you finish.

BUSHES, HEDGES, AND SMALL-TO-MEDIUM-SIZE EVERGREENS

Professionals prefer to use mini-lights with the random lighting technique mentioned on page 52 to decorate foliage. To do this, plug in your mini-lights and simply make patterns of lights, using no straight lines, until you've completely covered the plants evenly. If you've laid out multiple extension cords for larger hedges, make sure your separate light strands come together naturally. When working with pine trees, first plug in your mini-lights, then start from the top and work your way down. Don't forget your extension pole for the high places.

If you're using C7 or C9 strands, plug them in and test them first. Then unplug and hang them in the same manner as the mini-lights, plugging them in only after the lights are hung.

If you're using net lights, simply align the net on one end of the plant so that it's straight along the edge of your shrubbery. Once you have it lined up, gently stretch it over the sides and top. When it's covered, tuck the bottom of the net under the bush to help make it snug. Repeat this with the rest of your net lighting until the plant is completely covered.

SMALL TREETOPS
(6 TO 10 FEET)

If you're using mini-lights, plug them in and start putting the lights on limbs using the random lighting technique (see page 52). Work your way around the tree evenly and don't push the strands inside the branches. As you work, you may want to occasionally wrap the light strand around a branch to secure it to the tree so that it doesn't blow off during an arctic blast. Use your extension pole instead of trying to balance on a ladder.

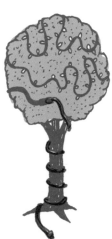

If you're using C7 or C9 strands, plug them in and test them first. Then unplug and hang them in the same manner as the mini-lights, plugging them in only after the lights are hung.

H I N T

Follow the manufacturer's directions on the package for the maximum number of lights you can string end to end.

MEDIUM AND
LARGE TREETOPS

With larger trees, you'll want to use the spiral lighting technique (see page 55). First plug in your mini-lights, and then wrap your light string a couple of times around the outer end of a bottom branch. This will hold the string in place. Now walk around the tree, moving the lights in an upward motion. Occasionally wrap the string around a branch to keep it from blowing off. Keep going all the way to the top of the tree—using an extension pole if necessary—spacing the light strands about a foot apart.

Using standard 100-bulb mini-light sets, you can usually string only three strands together. If you need more, you'll have to start back at the extension cord using a 3-way adapter, and fill in the area you have left.

If you're using C7 or C9 strands, follow the instructions for installation on small treetops (facing page).

TREE BRANCHES

If you decided to wrap individual branches instead of using the spiral technique (see the "Medium-Size Trees" section on page 55), refer back to your sketch to see how many mini-light strands you'll need. When wrapping branches, it's easier and faster to start with the lights strands wrapped up in a ball.

To do this, plug in your mini-lights and lay out the string on the grass. Starting with the female end, roll the whole string into a snug ball right up to the male end. Set it aside, and do the same with all the remaining light strings meant for your branches.

Of course, you can also have one of your helpers wrap the strings into balls while you begin wrapping the branches.

Okay, you have your light balls and you're ready to wrap. Now plug in a string and start wrapping the first branch, beginning at the trunk and working outward. Everyone will have a preference as to how close together they want their lights. Determine your personal taste and begin unwrapping the ball around the branch, going over and under.

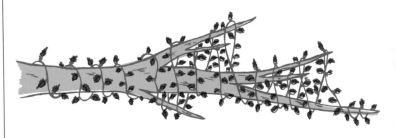

HINT

When wrapping branches and trunks, stay very consistent so that spacing is the same throughout the whole tree.

TREE TRUNKS

If you're wrapping your trunks with mini-light strings, as we recommend, prepare your lights with the light-ball technique described for branches (see page 81). When you're done rolling your balls, begin wrapping the trunk from the top and work your way down, leaving about six inches between each row of lights.

You'll want to wrap the trunks evenly, and tightly enough so that the light strings won't come loose or fall down. So put a little muscle into it—just not so much that you rip the lights apart. When you've wrapped the trunk all the way down, go back up in between the strands you've already wrapped. Repeat until you're satisfied with the number of lights on the trunk. When you're finished, tuck the loose female end under a line to hold the lights tight.

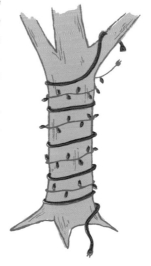

If you have net lighting for your trunks, wrap the netting tightly around the trunk, adding as many sets as needed to go all the way around the trunk. Then use the straps or hooks provided to hold the lights as tight as a belt buckle after an all-you-can-eat buffet.

FLOODLIGHTS AND SPOTLIGHTS

Floodlights and spotlights are sometimes sold in sets that include both a holder and a bulb; other times, these parts must be purchased separately. To set them up, stake your outdoor lamp holders into the ground, facing the direction in which you want your light to shine, and then screw in the bulb. If you're lighting a tree or other large single object, try to put lights on at least two sides to give the display some dimension.

HINT

It's easier to make adjustments in focusing your lights when it's dark.

LIGHT STAKES

Start your stakes as close to your power source as possible, to limit the number of extension cords you'll need to use. Snap your lights into the stakes before you begin inserting the stakes into the ground. Then, one by one, stake out your path along the driveway or walkway. Keep a screwdriver in your back pocket, too. You never know when you might come across a patch of hard

ground that will offer resistance. When that happens, just use the
screwdriver to begin a hole for your stake.

**It's important to keep the light lines and stakes as even and
straight as possible, as well as at a consistent height, so that
your finished job looks neat.**

STEP 3: HANG WREATHS, GARLAND, AND BOWS

WREATHS

Mark the spot where you want the top
of your wreath to be. Make sure it's
centered over the door, window, or
garage, and pick a spot high enough
that the wreath won't interfere with
opening doors.

Now insert a screw eye at your mark.
You'll need a slightly larger screw eye
than those you hung your lights with,
and you may need to drill a pilot hole.
After your screw eye is attached, use a
pair of pliers to open the eye wide
enough for the wreath frame to fit in.

Or you can attach wire to your wreath and hang it from that. It's your call.

If you'd like to hang the wreath on your door, there are special wreath holders designed for hanging wreaths off the top of doors (and screen doors). For windows, you can also use suction cups that have a hook in them, placing them firmly on the window itself and hanging your wreath on the hook.

Make sure to fluff the bow and check to make sure the lights work before hanging your wreath. Once it's hung, mark the place on the wall where the bottom of the wreath falls and install another screw eye there for support. Depending on the size of the wreath, you may want to install support on the sides, too.

HINT

Using a second screw eye at the bottom of the wreath frame will keep the wreath from scratching your home.

GARLAND

You'll want to hang garland so that it casually swags across the top and both ends hang down at an equal length. The easiest way to do this? Anchor two screw eyes over the top corners of the window or door.

Fold both ends of the garland together to find its center point, and mark it with a twist tie or piece of tape. Now, with one hand, hold the center of your garland over the center of the window or door. (The key to hanging garland is to have it perfectly centered.) Grab one side of the garland and attach it to a corner screw eye, leaving a little sway in the center. Repeat on the other side. For larger areas, you might need two people to complete this task—one person to hold the center and one to attach the corners.

Time to step back and take a look. Does the garland hang evenly on both sides? If not, fix it. When it's straightened out, add side anchors with more screw eyes. Start at the bottom and work your way up, placing an anchor every three feet or so. Side anchors may seem like overkill. But the morning you wake up and find that your garland has blown into your neighbor's shrubbery, you'll know why we suggested them.

Hanging garland over a garage or other long, horizontal expanse is just like hanging it over windows and doors, except that you're going to add a center screw eye. This eye will give you a double swag, which is more aesthetically pleasing for a

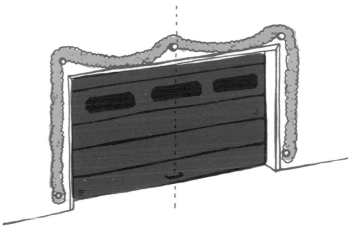

large area. When hanging, follow the previous directions: start at the center, make sure it hangs evenly, and then attach side anchors.

HINT

If your garland has lights and needs power, hang it so that the male plug is on the side closest to your power source.

NOTE

When attaching wreaths or garland to brick or stone, follow the directions in the sidebar "Attaching Lights to Brick or Stone" on page 77, using metal clips or plastic anchors and inserting screw eyes.

BOWS

Bows attached to wreaths and garland add a holiday touch to your home during the day, when your light display goes unseen. Installation is easy. Simply wrap some wire around the center of the bow and tie it to the greenery.

STEP 4: SET UP THE YARD ORNAMENTS

You could fill an entire book with all the different decorations available for your yard. But since we already have a book here, we'll just cover a few different types and their installation. Just remember, you'll want to make your yard decorations the focal point of your display.

PLASTIC LIGHT-UP ORNAMENTS

To help keep them from blowing into someone else's display, fill the bottoms with rocks or sand. You could also screw the ornament to a piece of wood a little larger than the ornament's base and use landscape nails to anchor the wood to the ground.

WIRE-FRAME ORNAMENTS

Most of these ornaments come with stakes to hold the display. If those aren't enough and you need a little more staying power, hammer a wooden stake into the ground and tie your ornament to that.

WOOD CUTOUTS

Hammer a wooden stake into the ground and attach the cutout to the stake with a single screw. This gives you the opportunity to straighten the cutout before adding an additional screw for support.

STEP 5: SET THE TIMERS

Finally, after you finish installing your display, it's time to add your timers. You'll need a timer at each outlet location being used. (If you have more than one timer for your display, getting them to come on simultaneously is tough.) Set your lights to come on just before dusk—that way, as the sun sets, you're set, too. Congratulations. You're done.

{ GARLAND AND WREATH *see page 72* }

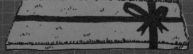

Chapter 4

TWELVE
PROJECTS

On the off-chance that the creative muse hasn't already struck you, here are twelve different decorating schemes to choose from. They're presented in order of difficulty, with #1 being the easiest and #12 being the hardest, but suffice it to say you can add and subtract elements to each—so if #11 strikes your fancy, tailor it to your desire. You can make each one of these as easy or as time-involved as you please.

#1 **EXPENSE:** *☆☆☆   **TIME:** *☆☆☆   **DIFFICULTY:** *☆☆☆

- -

SILENT NIGHT

Putting candles in the windows adds a nice, clean, classy look that will impress even your neighbors. And no, we are not talking about real candles —we are after the **plastic candles with a lightbulb at the top** that you plug in.

INSTRUCTIONS:

Count the number of windows you want to put a candle in—one candle for each. They can be placed in the front, side, and even the back of the home. Look for candles that have a light sensor, so all you have to do is place them in the window and plug them in. What the light sensor does is turn the candle on at dusk and off at dawn without you having to flip a switch or plug and unplug them every night. Finish off your display by placing a nice **wreath** on your front door, with a clear **floodlight** shining on it. If you have a screen door, it is best to place the wreath on the outside of it.

#2 EXPENSE: ** * * TIME: * * * * DIFFICULTY: * * * *

- -

LET IT SNOW, LET IT SNOW, LET IT SNOW

If snowflakes are your interest, why not turn your home into a wintry scene this holiday season? Yes, this will work even if you live in Florida.

INSTRUCTIONS:

Let's start with looking at your home and identifying locations where **artificial snowflakes** will fit. Snowflakes come in many different sizes, so you'll need to measure each area (height and width) where the snowflakes will be installed, and write this information down on a piece of paper. Don't forget to note any extension cords and timers you may need, too.

Finding snowflakes can be as easy as finding discount stores or home-improvement stores that sell Christmas decorations. The trick is finding the right snowflakes to fit in your designated areas.

Installing the snowflakes starts with first adding a screw eye at each of the locations you've chosen. If your house is made out of wood, the screw eye can be put directly into the outside of the house, in the center of the area where the snowflake will hang; if it's brick, see the "Attaching Lights to Brick or Stone" sidebar on page 77. Hang your snowflakes on the screw eyes and add extension cords. Install each snowflake, following the same process, until they are all hung. Now just plug them in, and you're set.

#3 EXPENSE: ****   TIME: ****   DIFFICULTY: ****

JINGLE BELLS

Looking for that perfect feel during the day and night for the holiday parties at your home this year? Well, this may be the style you are looking for—a little greenery for the daytime look, and some lights to give your home a nice, cozy feel at night.

INSTRUCTIONS:

Installing greenery will take a little while in the first year, but in subsequent years it will take just minutes. Let's start with getting some measurements of the location where you want to hang the **wreath**—we want to make sure our wreath will fit in the spot we have picked out. The goal is to get a wreath that is big enough to just fit into space you have planned. Now don't forget to measure the length of **garland** you need for around the door, too. After writing your measurements on a piece of paper, look at the bushes you want to light up. You'll need to decide on the types of **light strands** you want to use (minis, C7s, etc.) and what techniques you will use to install them (random, spiral, etc.), following the charts and information provided in chapter 3.

Start by installing the wreath with a screw eye as directed in this book, and then install the screw eyes for the garland—again following the instructions provided earlier. Now you can light up the bushes with your lights, installing them in a pattern to completely cover the bushes. Attach extension cords to the items needing power, plug them in a timer, and enjoy!

#4 EXPENSE: ***☆   TIME: **☆☆   DIFFICULTY: *☆☆☆

- -

CANDY CANE LANE

Looking to give your home a theme this year? Why not try Candy Cane Lane? Adding **red and clear miniature lights** on the bushes to match the **lighted candy canes** along the driveway is the finishing touch.

INSTRUCTIONS:

Let's start by looking at your home and figuring out how many candy canes you'll need to fill up the walkway and driveway. This is a matter of personal taste, but just make sure you have the same number of candy canes on each side to give a nice, balanced look. Now, for the bushes out front, you might have some luck finding light sets that have both red lights and clear lights. If not, you'll need to buy an equal number of red light sets and clear light sets to cover. Check the charts in the "Taking Measurements" section on page 52 to figure out how many sets you need for this project. Don't forget, you need to plug in all the decorations, too, so take that into account in figuring out how many extension cords you need.

Installing the candy canes is as simple as pushing them into the ground and plugging them into an extension cord. Just make sure to space them evenly and far enough away from the edge of the driveway that you won't hit them with the car door. For placing the lights on the bushes, just follow the installation instructions in Chapter 3.

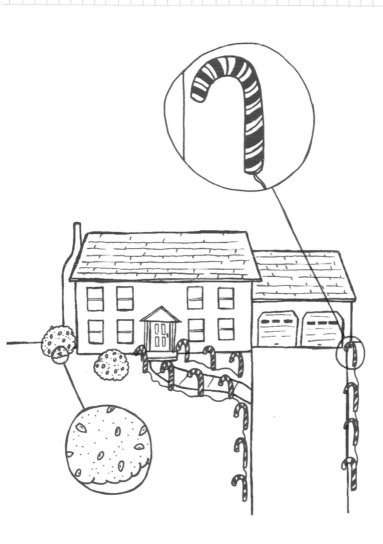

#5 EXPENSE: **✳✳ TIME: **✳✳ DIFFICULTY: *✳✳✳

MISTLETOE AND HOLLY

Trying to find that perfect holiday look to make everyone happy without spending a whole weekend installing decorations? If so, Mistletoe and Holly is for you. It has greenery for that warm feel, and some lights on the bushes for seasonal flair.

INSTRUCTIONS:

Grab your tape measure and measure the windows and the door where you want **wreaths** to hang. You always want to write down this information on a piece of paper to guarantee you buy the right quantity and sizes. Pictured here are wreaths with a nice big bow on them (no lights), but you can use lighted wreaths if you prefer.

Now let's look at the bushes that need **light strands**. Check the charts and information in the "Lights, Decorations, Action" section on page 30 to determine the styles and types of lights you will need, and write this information down on your shopping list, too. And don't forget about all the extension cords you will need for the bushes.

The wreaths will be hung, carefully centered, on the outsides of the windows. There are a couple of options for hanging them. The first is to install screw eyes in the centers of the window

continued ▶

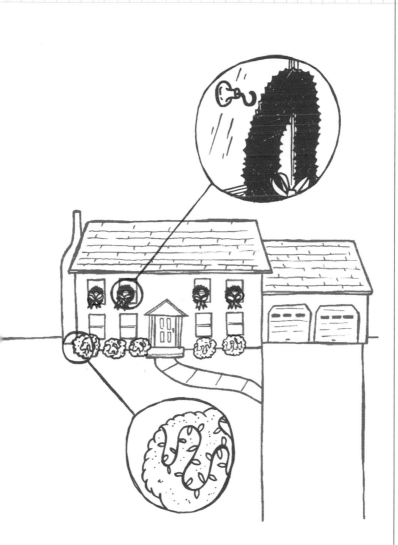

frames and hang the wreaths off them. Alternatively, you can use suction cups that have a hook in them, placing them firmly on the glass and hanging your wreath on the hook. (See page 85 for more on hanging wreaths on doors and windows.) For installing lights on the bushes, just follow the instructions in chapter 3. Finally, plug in your lights on the bushes and your display is finished.

#6 EXPENSE: ★★☆☆   TIME: ★★★☆   DIFFICULTY: ★★☆☆

OVER THE RIVER AND THROUGH THE WOODS

Many of us have real icicles hanging from our gutters during the winter season, but if you're someone who just wants to make icicles for yourself, this is for you. You'll get a shiver just seeing these lighted strings hanging from your eaves, without the water necessary to make the real thing. Adding some lights to your pine trees and bushes will finish off the display, giving it a complete look.

INSTRUCTIONS:

First things first. Measure the total length of the trim where you want your **icicle lights** to hang, writing this information down on a piece of paper. Now look at the bushes and pines that will be getting **light strands** and figure out the best styles for hanging them (random, spiral, etc.) and the types of lights you want to use (minis, C7s, etc.). Go back and look at the chart on page 54 to see how many light strands you'll need. If your pines are too high to light easily from the ground, you might need an extension pole (see page 27). When buying your icicles, check the box for the length of each section and compare that to the measurements you've written on your shopping list. *continued* ▶

When you install the icicles on the trim of your house, start from the end nearest the power source. You will probably need to use an extension cord and run it up the side of the house to the edge of the gutter to plug in your first set of icicles. Remember, you can usually plug in only three sets of icicles end to end; additional sets will need to be plugged into another power source. This means you might have to run an extension cord along the gutter from the main power source where you plugged in your first set of icicles. Once the icicle lights are up and working, you can start installing the light strands on the bushes and pines, as directed in chapter 3. Plug all your lights in and make any adjustment to the lights on the pines and bushes so they are covered evenly. A word of advice: make your final adjustment of the lights at dusk so you can see any open areas that still need illumination.

#7 EXPENSE: ****   TIME: ****   DIFFICULTY: ****

O CHRISTMAS TREE!

You must have a nice-looking display if you plan on having Santa standing in your yard for the holidays. O Christmas Tree! adds a little height by placing bigger bulbs on the trim and two lighted artificial trees by the front door.

INSTRUCTIONS:

Determine the length of the trim and note it on your shopping list. Use your measuring tape to measure all the areas you want to illuminate. Next, decide on the types and colors of the **light strands** you want to use. For installing the lights on the trim, follow the instructions in the "Roofline" section on page 72.

Now install your **inflatable Santa**. Find a good location in the yard that will be the focal point, and place your Santa there. Always follow the installation instructions from the manufacturer. A couple of **artificial trees** for the front door are next. Sometimes it's better to go with thin trees that are prelit—installation is simple, and there will be enough room for people to come and go from your home. Placing the trees in separate pots will give your display a nice, clean look and will hold the trees up during windy days. After you unpack your trees, put them together and place each tree and its stand in the pot (make sure to get a pot that is big enough for the stand). Now you need some weights to help hold the trees upright. You can use rocks or sand-

bags for this job—anything that is heavy and will hold the trees in place. Finally, plug in all your decorations and set the timer(s).

#8 EXPENSE: ★★★☆   TIME: ★★★☆   DIFFICULTY: ★★☆☆

DECK THE HALLS

This project lets you bring a little wildlife into your front yard—well, at least a wire-frame deer with a bunch of Christmas lights on it. Just make sure that the deer-hunting season is over before you set up.

INSTRUCTIONS:

Start with the **garland** for the house, measuring around the front door to determine what length garland you need. Then measure the area around the garage, where the other section of garland will go. Now count the number of **bows** needed for the garland, usually one per corner. You will need to go back to the section on branch wrapping (see page 55) to find out how many **light strands** you'll need for your project. As for the **lighted wire deer**, there are different sizes and colors to choose from—surely one will appeal to your personal taste. Most places that sell Christmas decorations sell these wire-frame deer.

Follow the instructions in chapter 3 for installing the garland and wrapping the lights on the tree. Follow the instructions on the package for setting up the deer, making sure the deer is set in a good location in the yard where everyone can see it. Now just plug in your extension cords and make any necessary final adjustments.

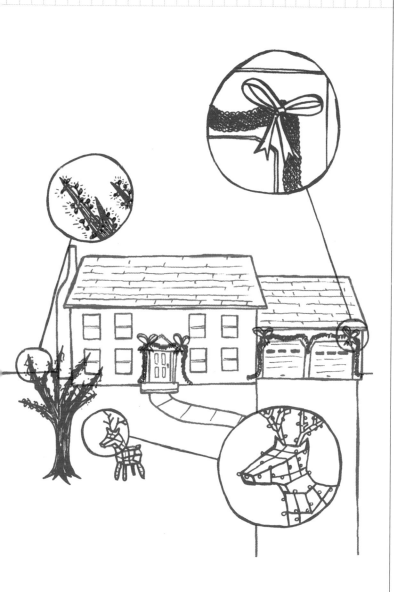

#9 EXPENSE: ★★★☆   TIME: ★★★☆   DIFFICULTY: ★★★☆

- -

WHITE CHRISTMAS

Planning to compete in this year's annual neighborhood decorating contest? Well, White Christmas just might take first place.

INSTRUCTIONS:

You will need to take a couple of measurements before you get started with this project, so grab that measuring tape and let's go. First thing is measuring the total length of the area where you are hanging your decorations from the trim. Next, you'll need to measure the total length of the **light strands** you'll be putting on light stakes. Make sure to write down all this information on a piece of paper. Finally, figure out the lighting you need for the trees. See the "Taking Measurements" section on page 52 for details. Don't forget that you will need lights (C7 or C9 strings) for the stake lighting, as well as stake light holders, extension cords, and timers.

Now it's installation time! You want to start by running an extension cord up the corner of the house to the gutter where the **hanging decorations** will start. Begin at that corner, hanging the decorations from the gutter, and continue across the trim to the end. You might have to run up a couple of extension cords to cover all the areas where the stars are hanging. To attach them, you can use plastic clips, available where Christmas lights are sold.

When installing the stake lights, start by first inserting the bulbs into the stake holders, and then push those into the ground, starting at the front door and working your way down the drive-

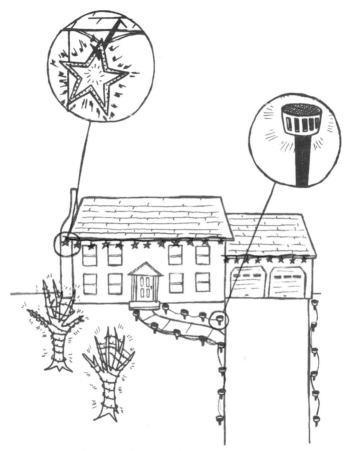

way. Just make sure when installing them that the stakes are in a straight line and all at the same height.

Now, let's move on to the two lighted trees out front. Use the spiral lighting technique for them, following the instructions on page 55. Finish up by running any extra extension cords where you might need them, and plug in the display.

#10 EXPENSE: *** TIME: *** DIFFICULTY: ***

RUDOLPH THE RED-NOSED REINDEER

If you've just moved into your new home and are looking to impress the neighbors this holiday season, Rudolph is designed especially for you.

INSTRUCTIONS:

Let's start with a pencil and paper and a measuring tape. The first thing you want to do is measure the trim of the house where you'll be installing the **C9 light sets**. You just need an approximate length. Write this information on the paper. Next, measure the height and width of the area where the **wreath** is going and the spot you've picked for your **"Happy Holidays" sign**. Once again, write down these measurements. Now, looking at your walkway, determine how many **trees** should go in the space you have. Also check where the outlets are and make a list of the extension cords you'll need. The **lighted snowman**, the **Santa**, and the **reindeer** come in many different styles and sizes. You'll want to purchase those that will best fit your display.

Start your installation with the trim of the house, followed by the wreath and the "Happy Holidays" sign. The C9 strings for the trim can be attached to the gutters with plastic clips; if you don't have a gutter, slide the clips under the shingles. You will need to

continued ▶

run an extension cord up to the C9 strings and start there. The wreath and sign can be hung from screw eyes, which can be found at a home-improvement store. Walkway trees just need to be pushed into the ground and plugged in (if you're lighting them). Just make sure they are evenly spaced along the walkway. Your snowman, Santa, and reindeer can be placed right on the grass. Some outdoor displays have poles that allow you simply to push them into the ground. If you're not sure how to secure your yard decorations, check the packaging or instructions that came with them. After everything is installed, plug in all the extension cords and set the timers.

#11 EXPENSE: ****   TIME: ****   DIFFICULTY: ****
- -

AWAY IN A MANGER

If you're looking to dress up and play Santa for all the kids visiting your display, Away in a Manger is for you.

INSTRUCTIONS:

We have a lot of **garland** for this project, and that will be the place to start your shopping checklist. Grab your paper and pencil, and let's start by measuring the trim of the house where you'll be hanging the garland. You will need a little extra garland for each swag you install, so add 10 percent to the total length you measure. Next is the garland for over the driveway. Using your measuring tape, measure the distance across the driveway, making sure to leave about two feet on each side of the driveway so you have room to open your car doors. Now add 10 percent to that measurement for the sag, and that should give you a good estimate for this section. Multiply that length by three, since there are three garland swags on the driveway.

For example, say the distance across your driveway is 16 feet. You'll need to add 2 feet on each side (extra space for car doors and snow), which gives you a total of 20 feet (16 + 4). Now add 10 percent to that total (extra length for the sag when the garland is hung over the drive), or 2 feet, and you get a total length of 22 feet for one section of garland across the drive. If you're planning on hanging three sections of garland, multiply

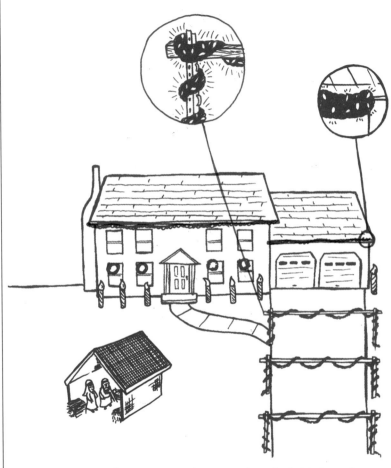

22 x 3, and you'll come up with a grand total of 66 feet of garland needed for the driveway.

You will need something to hold up the garland over the driveway, too. Using **metal T-posts** and hammering them into the ground is going to be your best bet. After the T-posts are in the ground, you can attach a **10-foot-tall 2x4 wood piece** to the T-post by wiring the wood securely to the T-post, and attach your garland to the top of the 2x4. These supplies can be purchased at your local home-improvement store—make sure to put them on your list.

Next, measure your windows to determine what size **wreaths** you'll need to get. As for the **blow-mold candles**, look at your home and see how many would best complement your display, and write that number on your shopping list. Last, think about your **nativity scene**. These come in many different sizes and styles— choose the one that best fits your yard and your budget.

Installation should start with the garland on the trim of the house. If you're using a lighted garland, you will need to run an extension cord up the side of the house to plug in your greenery. When installing the garland, try to make sure all the sags are the same length. Hang the wreaths on the windows by installing a screw eye at the top center of each window. Next, install the garland over the driveway; first install the T-posts on both sides, then attach a 10-foot-tall 2x4 wood piece by wiring the 2x4 to the T-post vertically, making sure that you have the 2x4 securely fastened. Now all you have to do is screw or nail the garland to the top of the 2x4 on both sides. Make sure the section of wood is high enough off the ground that you can drive your car beneath it. Last, install your nativity scene at a good focal point in the yard, following the manufacturer's instructions. Plug in everything with extension cords and test all the lights.

#12 EXPENSE: **** TIME: **** DIFFICULTY: ****

WINTER WONDERLAND

If you are looking to make the front page of the newspaper for best display in your community, it's Winter Wonderland time. It is sure to put a smile on all the children's faces, and even the adults', too.

INSTRUCTIONS:

Let's start by assembling the list of supplies you'll need for this project. First, measure your house's trim and the windows to see what lengths **light strands** you'll need. Make sure to write this information on your shopping list. Measure completely around each window. If all your windows are the same size, you just need to multiply the measurements from one window by the total number of windows to know how many sets of lights you will need. If your windows are different sizes, you will need to measure each one and write all that information down. Now do the same thing around the door and around the garage. When you go shopping, remember that light sets come in varying lengths—check the boxes to make sure the strands are the right length for your intended application. Too long is fine; it's better than too short. You must also think about how you're going to install these lights. If you're attaching them to the windows inside the house, you will need clips that have self-sticking tabs on them. If you're planning to

continued ▶

install them around the outside of the windows, you will need screw eyes. Just keep this in mind when you go shopping. The last thing you'll need for the house itself is a **wreath** to hang on the front door.

Place **trees with lights** on them and **gift packages** on the ground in the yard. Both the trees and the gift packages come in several different styles (metal or plastic) and many different sizes. Some trees come prelit, and others require you to install your own lights. Check your local department stores to see what is available. The quantity needed for your display will be determined by the sizes of the trees and gift packages, and how much yard you have available.

After purchasing all the necessary supplies for your display, you will want to start the installation by putting up the lights on the trim of the house and the windows. To get power up to the trim for the lights, start by running your extension cord to the trim, ideally hiding it behind a drainpipe. Then plug in your lights and install them. If your windows are up high, use the same method of getting the extension cord to the windows, by running it up the drainpipe. For lower windows, you can just plug your lights into the extension cord and drop the cord straight down to the ground where you can plug it into a power supply. You will do the same for window lights, wrapping any extra lights around each window. Now for the door and garage, start on the side closest to your power source. Hanging the lights from screw eyes is your best bet. Hang the wreath on the door with either a wreath hook that slips over the door, or, if you prefer, hammer a small nail into the door and place the wreath on the nail.

Place the trees and gift packages where they'll be in full view from the street, and in such a way that they fill up the yard evenly. Follow the instructions that came with these displays for proper installation. Now comes the time to install all the extension cords and plug in the rest of your display, making any adjustments you see fit.

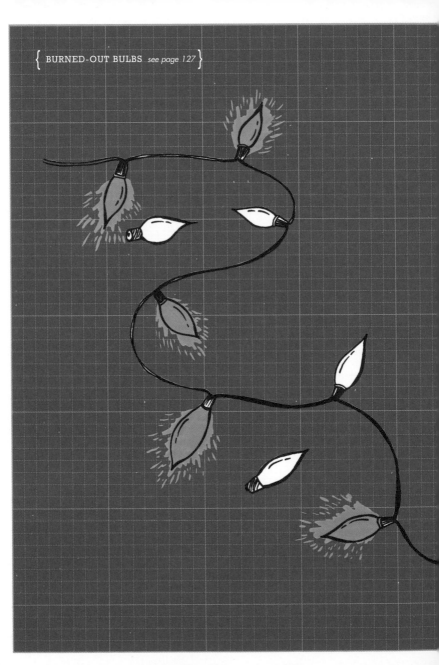

{ BURNED-OUT BULBS *see page 127* }

Chapter 5

TROUBLE-
SHOOTING

If you've read through this entire book and you still have a question or a problem that you don't have a solution to, this is your section.

PROBLEM: I have an entire string of lights out.

SOLUTION: First check for a bad connection by wiggling the plug a little. Not it? Check the fuse in the male end of the plug to see if it's blown. Still nothing? Look for missing or bad bulbs.

PROBLEM: I have a set of lights that blink off and on when I touch them.

SOLUTION: You have yourself a loose bulb or connection. While the strand is plugged in, cup your hand and run it slowly along the string. When the strand blinks, you've found the bulb. Just replace it. By running your hand over the light string, you are helping the bad bulb make contact with the wires in the strand, triggering the blinking. Once you replace the bad bulb in question, make sure you also replace any burned-out bulbs. There will be times where you come across just one bulb that's not making good contact and will only need to replace that one. Other times, several bulbs will need replacing.

PROBLEM: Only half the lights on my 100-bulb mini-light string are on.

SOLUTION: Because mini-lights are wired in two 50-light series, one bad bulb can make half your bulbs go out. So what you have is a bulb that's either burned out or is not making contact in the socket. First, check the section where the lights are out and look for cut wires and or missing bulbs. If everything looks okay, plug the lights in and run your hand over the sections back and forth to help wiggle the lightbulbs. The majority of the time, wiggling the string of lights will make it light up—and then you can identify those bulbs that need replacing.

PROBLEM: How many C7 or C9 strands can be plugged end to end?
SOLUTION: Three sets, for a total of 75 feet. Just follow the manufacturer's directions.

PROBLEM: I have a few burned-out bulbs, but the rest of the string is working. Do I need to replace the bulbs?
SOLUTION: Absolutely. If you get a couple more burned-out bulbs, the whole strand may go. Better to replace the bulbs you know are out now than to have to search the entire strand later.

PROBLEM: There's not enough power from an outlet on the front of the house to run all the lights.
SOLUTION: Get some long extensions cords and use outlets in the backyard or garage. If you're really serious, call an electrician and he or she can install a new outlet.

PROBLEM: My GFCI tripped.
SOLUTION: Chances are, your outdoor lights or extension cords have moisture in them. First, you need to find the tripped GFCI outlet and try to reset it. If it's wet outside, it could take a day or two for the standing moisture in the lines to dry up enough for the GFCI to reset. Second, check all your light strands and extension cord connections to make sure they're not lying in

water. Gutters are a good place to start, because rain is the number one cause of tripping. When you find the wet cords or strands, allow them to dry before resetting the GFCI.

PROBLEM: The breaker in my electrical panel won't stay on when I reset it.

SOLUTION: You have too many cords plugged into this circuit. You'll have to move some cords to another outlet not on this circuit. You should also check the cords outside to see if any animals have chewed through them or if lines are cut.

PROBLEM: The elves won't do what they're told.

SOLUTION: You're on your own for this one, Mr. Claus.

{ STORAGE OPTIONS *see page 135* }

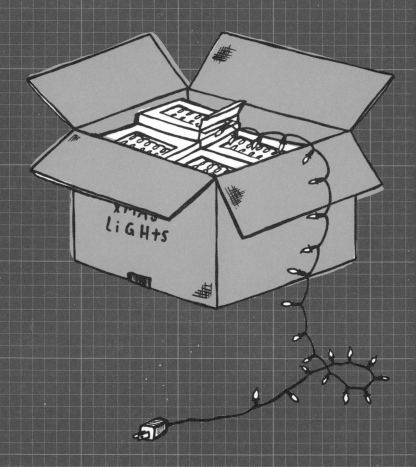

Chapter 6

TAKEDOWN
AND STORAGE

You cooked the goose. You opened the gifts. You toasted the New Year. The bowl games are over. It's time to take down your display. Hopefully it's not yet St. Patrick's Day. While you don't want to tackle subzero temperatures or black ice just to get your holiday lights off the house, you don't want to need suntan lotion either. That said, let's get started. Get out your favorite post-holiday beverage and break out the Holiday Hero Tool Kit. Baseball's just around the corner.

ADD TO YOUR MAIN SKETCH

You have your photos. Now make sure your sketch is thorough. Don't waste time next season trying to figure out everything you did this year. Write it all down on your sketch, and it will all be clear.

ELECTRICAL

Use a pen to draw your extension cord layout. Your sketch should be detailed enough to show which outlets were used, where connections were made, and what colors the cords are.

LIGHTS

Next to each feature in your display, write down:

- Total number of lights used for each feature
- How the lights were installed (spiral, random, etc.)
- What types of lights were used and what colors

TAKE A PICTURE

Stop. Don't take anything down. Nothing. Not until you've taken a picture with the lights on. Wait until dusk. That way, the lights will show up and there will still be enough light for the camera to work. You might want to take several pictures to get in your entire display. The more pictures you have, the faster and easier next year's setup will be.

TAKE IT DOWN

- Don't worry about storing your lights exactly as they were bought from the store. Wrap and package them in the way that's easiest for you. For storing miniature-light strings, just wrap them up like you would your extension cords, around your arm.

- If you wrapped tree branches or tree trunks, go ahead and take the light strings down by winding them into balls so they're ready to use next year. Just make sure when you wrap them up that the male plug is on the outside of the ball so you can test it next year.

- Never store your lights while they're still wet. This will rust the connections and ruin the lights and cords. If you take down all your lights and decorations and they are still wet, wait till they dry out before packing them up for storage. This might take a day or two.

- Leave plastic clips attached to light strings. No need to undo all your hard work.

- Put your greenery and bows in a nice sturdy plastic bin or box so you don't crush the branches or the lights.

- Whatever you do, put your sketch, pictures, and notes in one of your containers so they can be easily found next season. Losing all that hard work would be, well, not very smart.

- Don't remove the screw eyes. Consider these as part of a permanent installation to be used for other holiday decorations, too.

STORE IT

When storing your lights and decorations, find a nice, clean, dry area where they will be safe to sit an entire year. Cover your larger decorations with trash bags, or use a painter's drop cloth to help protect them from dust. Label each box or tub ("Christmas Decorations"), and note specifically what is inside.

Now you're all set for next year. It's okay to start decorating after Halloween, right?

ABOUT THE AUTHOR

For more than 20 years, Brad Finkle has decorated the homes and businesses of the Midwest. You could easily mistake his business references for a Fortune magazine list. Season after season, his clients refer him to their friends, so he now spends his entire year creating and producing elements for the next season's displays. Past displays have won numerous awards from the Illuminating Engineering Society of North America. Visit his Web site at www.creativedecoratinginc.com. And no, he doesn't decorate his own yard. After all, do you think a chef cooks for himself when he gets home from work?